Kim and Mario Walk
Labyrinths and So Can You

Also By Kim Antieau

Novels

The Blue Tail • Broken Moon • Butch
Church of the Old Mermaids • Coyote Cowgirl
Deathmark • The Desert Siren • The Fish Wife
The Gaia Websters • Her Frozen Wild
Jewelweed Station • The Jigsaw Woman
Killing Beauty • Mercy, Unbound
The Monster's Daughter
Queendom: Feast of the Saints
Ruby's Imagine • Swans in Winter • The Rift
Whackadoodle Times • Whackadoodle Times Two •
Whackadoodle Times Three

Nonfiction

Answering the Creative Call • Certified
Counting on Wildflowers
Kim and Mario Build a Labyrinth and So Can You
Magic, Myth, and Merrymaking: 13 Days of Yuletide
the Old Mermaids Way
The Old Mermaids Book of Days and Nights
The Salmon Mysteries
Spirits, Spells and Storytelling: 13 Days of Hallows
the Old Mermaids Way • Under the Tucson Moon

Short Story Collections

Entangled Realities (with Mario Milosevic)
The First Book of Old Mermaids Tales
Tales Fabulous and Fairy
Trudging to Eden

Also By Mario Milosevic

Novels
Claypot Dreamstance
The Coma Monologues
The Doctor and the Clown
Kyle's War
The Last Giant
Splitting
Terrastina and Mazolli

Collections
A Bestiary of Imaginary Species
Entangled Realities (with Kim Antieau)
Labor Days
Miniatures
Mostly Invisible
20 Strange Tales of Crime and Mystery

Poetry
Alien Life
Animal Life
Bugs
Fantasy Life
Love Life
Mario Writes a Poem a Day for a Year and so Can You

Kim and Mario Walk Labyrinths and So Can You

Kim Antieau and Mario Milosevic

Kim and Mario Walk Labyrinths and So Can You
by Kim Antieau and Mario Milosevic

Copyright © 2024 by Kim Antieau and Mario Milosevic

ISBN: 978-1-949644-86-9

Photos by Kim Antieau and Mario Milosevic except for the Grace Cathedral on page 29 which is from Depositphotos. Diagram of Classical labyrinth also from Depositphotos. Diagram of Medieval labyrinth by Mario Milosevic.

Thanks to Nancy Milosevic

All rights reserved. No part of this book may be copied without permission of the authors.

Published by Green Snake Publishing.
www.greensnakepublishing.com

Contents

At the Threshold — 9

Stepping onto the Path — 15

Types of Labyrinths — 19

How to Walk a Labyrinth — 21

Kim & Mario Walk Labyrinths — 27

Grace Cathedral, San Francisco, California — 29

The Grotto Labyrinth, Portland, Oregon — 31

Labyrinth at the Menucha Retreat and Conference Center, Corbett, Oregon — 33

Cretan Labyrinth at Trout Lake Abbey/White Mountain Druid Sanctuary, Trout Lake, Washington — 35

Mabel Dodge Luhan House Labyrinth, Taos, New Mexico — 37

Labyrinth at Ghost Ranch Conference Center, Abiquiu, New Mexico — 39

Sacred Heart Parish Labyrinth, Anderson, California — 41

Beth Shalom Temple Center, Green Valley, Arizona — 43

Boyce Thompson Arboretum, Superior, Arizona — 45

Corpus Christi Catholic Church, Tucson, Arizona — 47

Episcopal Church of St. Matthew, Tucson, Arizona — 49

Franciscan Renewal Center, Scottsdale, Arizona — 51

Grace St. Paul's Episcopal Church, Tucson, Arizona	53
Prestige Assisted Living at Green Valley, Arizona	55
St. Francis in the Valley Episcopal Church, Green Valley, Arizona	57
Highland Vista Neighborhood Association, Tucson, Arizona	59
Immanuel Presbyterian Church, Tucson, Arizona	61
Episcopal Church of the Apostles, Oro Valley, Arizona	63
Rio Vista Natural Resource Park, Tucson, Arizona	65
Sanctuary Cove Labyrinth, Base of Tucson Mountains, Arizona	67
St John on the Desert Presbyterian Church, Tucson, AZ	69
Saint Philip's in the Hills, Tucson, Arizona	71
Sunrise Chapel Labyrinth, Tucson, Arizona	73
Rincon Congregational United Church of Christ, Tucson, Arizona	75
Unity of Tucson, Tucson, Arizona	77
The Old Mermaids Sanctuary Labyrinth	79
About the Authors	81

At the Threshold

Kim grew up in the country in southeast Michigan following paths wildlife made through the woods and along the banks of the Huron River; Mario spent most of his childhood in a mining town in Canada tracing paths the stars made in the sky.

Like most humans, we were and are pathfinders, looking for ways to navigate our lives and find the best way forward. In our adulthood, together, we became intrigued by one path in particular: the path of the labyrinth.

Kim's interest in labyrinths started after she got labyrinthitis, an infection of the inner ear which caused severe vertigo. The doctor told her she would just have to wait it out; it would eventually get better. She looked up the meaning of the word labyrinth and rediscovered the tale of King Minos having Daedalus create a maze to trap the Minoan Bull. This maze was called a labyrinth (even though nowadays a labyrinth has one way in and one way out). In her illness, she often felt trapped—like the Minoan Bull.

Kim looked for any information she could find on labyrinths. Elinor Gadon in *The Once and Future Goddess* wrote about the labyrinth as the body of the goddess. The patriarchy rewrote the stories and turned the Minoan Bull evil and had Theseus come into the labyrinth and cruelly kill him. But before that, essentially, the labyrinth was woman.

Archeologist Marija Gimbutas frequently found labyrinths on her digs. She believed they represented the Great Goddess as powerful, full of life, and full of the ability to exact death.

According to Monica Sjoo and Barbara Mor writing in their book *The Great Cosmic Mother: Rediscovering the Religion of the Earth*, labyrinths were always connected with a cave or womb, and "presided over by mythical women." The labyrinth protected the heart of the ones who came forth, going in and going out. They described women purposefully dancing the labyrinth in a ritual of life, death, and rebirth.

Kim also read Lauren Artress's *Walking a Sacred Path: Rediscovering the Labyrinth as a Spiritual Practice*. She learned ancient artists had depicted labyrinths on rocks, coins, and tiles as far back as 4,000 years ago, all over the world.

The idea that people had been creating labyrinths and then in some places walking them for thousands of years was intriguing. Kim wondered if she could walk into a labyrinth, find healing, and walk back out again.

Kim felt compelled to make labyrinths, so we made a labyrinth in the sand on a beach in Oregon during a visit and watched the tide wash it away. We also made one out of string—a small one—in our yard in Stevenson, Washington, when we lived there.

Artress wrote about the labyrinths in Grace Cathedral in San Francisco where the modern labyrinth movement began. Kim decided she had to walk that labyrinth. Maybe she could find healing there.

So we drove from the Columbia River Gorge in Washington to the Grace Cathedral in San Francisco. We walked into the church, full of excitement and hope. We remember it was dark inside. Kim had never been in a church that wasn't Catholic, and she was surprised by the lack of art and iconography.

She stepped up to the opening of the labyrinth and began walking. She waited for some kind of sign or beam of light or something profound. Instead her mind raced, telling her all kinds of awful things about what was wrong with her. Mario remembers the high ceiling and the echos that seemed to careen from wall to wall.

We walked the outside labyrinth, too. It was made of stone, and Kim liked walking it. She remembers either the sound of traffic or the wind as we walked, yet it felt freeing being outside.

Nothing much changed in our lives once we walked our first labyrinth made by someone else, but after being sick for such a long time, Kim felt buoyed by her ability to take such a long and somewhat grueling trip. Maybe life could go on with some normalcy and adventure.

After that, we began walking labyrinths wherever we could find them. This was before the World-Wide Labyrinth Locator came into existence, yet we found labyrinths now and again. Once the World-Wide Labyrinth Locator was in place, it was much easier. When we traveled, the first thing we checked after getting to our lodging was how to find the nearest labyrinth.

In the beginning, Mario worried that he was missing something. "I don't feel anything change," he would sometimes say. He thought he should be having a profound transformation, but it never seemed to arrive.

Kim stopped looking for enlightenment or healing when walking. Instead, for her, it became a kind of meditation, a way of being calm and grounded for a time. The rhythm of walking the labyrinth became part of the rhythm of our lives.

When we moved to Arizona in 2019 and bought some acreage, one of the first things we did was build an 11-circuit Chartres-style labyrinth in a bull pen in our back pasture. We even wrote a book about it to help other people build their own labyrinth: *Kim and Mario Build a Labyrinth and So Can You*. A year later, we built a Cretan Classical labyrinth next to the Chartres one.

Our own labyrinths are our favorites, of course, but we continue to walk other labyrinths, and we'll explore some of those here.

Stepping onto the Path

We occasionally host writers, artists, and other travelers on our property. Most of the time, our visitors have no idea what a labyrinth is or what they should or can do with it. If that's the case with you, too, as you are reading this book, have no worries. We knew very little about labyrinths ourselves at one time. We all have to begin somewhere. This book is as good a place as any to begin.

At one time a labyrinth and a maze were the same thing. Not any longer. A maze is designed to trick. There is not one way in and out. That is the difference. The labyrinth is a path, a way, a pilgrimage, a walk: one way in and one way out. No tricks and little chance of getting lost or losing your way.

Nowadays, a labyrinth is a pattern that is usually a circle but can be a square, octagon, or any other shape. It has a single path that winds to the center. All the labyrinths we write about here are walkable and people walk them for all kinds of reasons: to connect with themselves, Nature, the divine, their creativity, or just to have a stroll.

What did they symbolize to people 4,000 years ago? We have no idea. We don't even know if they existed on land or if the patterns were only depicted on tiles, walls, and rocks.

Because they existed before organized religions as we know them today, labyrinths are essentially pagan. We have little idea what they meant to ancient people.

By the Middle Ages, many Christian churches had labyrinths in them. Some scholars believe they were used during those times as a way of "walking a pilgrimage" when one couldn't afford (or didn't want) to travel to Jerusalem on pilgrimage. The Chartres Cathedral with its now famous labyrinth was constructed in 1200 CE.

Rabbi Jill Hammer writes in *My Jewish Learning* that "Jews have long related to the labyrinth as an experience of journey or pilgrimage. We find the labyrinth as an illustration in Jewish texts, including the Taj Torah, a 15th-century Hebrew manuscript from Yemen, which features the six-circuit Jericho labyrinth depicting the Israelites conquering the city across a labyrinthine path." Because the labyrinth is found in Jewish texts, she says this suggests "they are meant to be sacred."

In almost any place and in any culture, if one does a little digging, one can find evidence of ancient labyrinths. For instance in the Casa Grand Monument ruins in Arizona, a labyrinth that looks very much like the labyrinth on Cretan coins was incised on a third story wall. Although historical evidence indicates this labyrinth is pre-Columbian, no one knows for certain. Several labyrinths are depicted on rocks throughout the Southwest United States, but no one knows when they were created or by whom.

So we don't know much—if anything—about how our ancestors used labyrinths, but in places all over the world today, people from all kinds of backgrounds of different faiths and spiritualities—or no faiths or spiritualities—walk labyrinths.

Mario walks them because it's a "me and you thing," he says. He does it because we do it together. Kim likes walking them because we've walked labyrinths for 30 years or more together, and it's a way for her to ground and be calm in a world that often feels too chaotic for her.

Types of Labyrinths

Although there are different patterns to labyrinths, the Classical or Cretan Labyrinth and the 11-circuit Medieval Labyrinth are the ones we come across most often—and they are the ones we've built on our property.

The oldest known labyrinth is the 7-circuit Classical labyrinth found on a clay tablet from the ruins in Pylos in Greece. It dates back to around 1200 BCE.

We often think of the Classical or Cretan design as the more wild labyrinth and the one that feels more natural, but that's just us! The Cretan/Classical labyrinths also have 3, 5, 7, 11, and 15-circuit designs.

The 11-circuit Medieval labyrinth is the pattern of

the Chartres Cathedral. They don't know for certain when the labyrinth was laid down, but it was probably during that first decade of the 13th century. This labyrinth comes in 5- and 7-circuit variations.

Classical/Cretan Design

Medieval Design

How to Walk a Labyrinth

Millions of people around the world walk labyrinths every day. On the labyrinth locator, (google it) you can now find over 6,000 labyrinths.

As far as we're concerned, there is no right or wrong way to walk a labyrinth. However, we have some suggestions to help make the walk more meaningful and more comfortable.

Before we give those suggestions, however, we want to mention that we understand people have different abilities. In this book, we are writing about how *we* walk labyrinths. What we are able to do or not able to do can be different from what someone else is able to do. We hope you can take our experiences and suggestions and adjust them to fit your needs and abilities.

So . . .

Before you start walking a labyrinth, you might want to ask yourself why you are walking. Is it because it's there? Because you have an issue you're wrestling with? Because you need to relax? Because you want to connect with yourself, Nature, or the divine? Because you enjoy it? Is walking a labyrinth a pilgrimage for you?

Don't judge whatever your reason is. There is no right or wrong answer to these questions. It can just enrich your experience to know why you are walking the labyrinth.

Ask a Question

If you have a problem, and you're trying to figure it out, you might ask a question before stepping into the labyrinth. Form the question, keep it in your mind, but don't obsess over it. Take a deep breath, feel your feet on the ground, and then step onto the path and walk.

By the time you get to the center of the labyrinth, you may have a solution. Or you may get the answer later. Even if you never get an answer, you may have more clarity on the issue than you did when you started once you have completed your walk.

Recite a Mantra

If you're a worrier or your mind wanders a lot, you might want to recite a mantra to yourself as you walk. You can try OM or OM AH HUM. Or the word "peace." Or recite a prayer or a poem. This can keep unwanted thoughts at bay while you walk, and it can help you relax.

Connect

If you are trying to connect with yourself or the divine or the universe, keep an open mind. Be in the labyrinth. Be observant. It can be beneficial to let go of any expectations and accept what the labyrinth gives you. Just see what happens.

Think of It As a Pilgrimage

Perhaps your labyrinth walk is a pilgrimage. A pilgrimage has often come to mean a journey to a sacred or holy place. But it can be any kind of journey. The word pilgrim means stranger or traveler. So a pilgrimage is a journey. Kim thinks of every walk in a labyrinth as a type of pilgrimage. For her, a pilgrimage is a journey where we stay awake, where we are as fully present as we can be, where we leave our expectations behind and adopt the beginner's mind. We travel on the path; we find the center; then we return home.

What to Leave Behind

Take as little as possible with you. Leave your phone behind or at least turn it off. Leave your expectations behind. If it's hot and or sunny, bring water and wear a hat.

Consider Adopting the Beginner's Mind

Beginner's mind is a Zen Buddhism concept called *shoshin*. It is a beautiful way of letting go of expectations and looking at every experience or each activity with an open mind, as if all of it is a new experience. Shunryu Suzuki wrote in his book *Zen Mind, Beginner's Mind*, "If your mind is empty, it is always ready for anything, it is open to everything. In the beginner's mind there are many possibilities, but in the expert's there are few."

Ready?

Now that You Have Prepared

Stand at the entrance to the labyrinth. Take a deep breath. Feel your feet on the ground. Step onto the path and begin to walk. You are now in the container. You can imagine whatever you want or nothing at all. If you have a question, say it to yourself. If you have a mantra or prayer, say it to yourself. Be open. We find it's best to walk a labyrinth in silence, especially if others are walking with you.

What Happens At the Center

Keep walking until you reach the center. Once there, you can turn around and start back the way you came if you like. But staying in the center—literally staying centered—is always a nice choice.

When Kim gets to the center, she honors the goddess Sovereignty. She is the goddess of the land; she is the land. In Celtic Ireland, all rulers had to behave in a way that honored Sovereignty—in ways that honored and protected the land through "righteous behavior." Kim feels a deep connection to the land, to the Earth, and so here she honors Sovereignty.

When Mario arrives at the center he usually pauses and then faces the four directions in turn: East, North, West, and South. He stretches his arms out at his sides and spreads his hands and takes mental note of his surroundings whether it is mountains, fields, trees, buildings, or clouds.

What you do is up to you, of course.

The Petals

The six petals surrounding the center of a Medieval style labyrinth are often called rose petals. (The Cretan labyrinth doesn't have these petals.) To us, it doesn't look like any rose we've seen. It's more like a daisy. In any case, we've read in various places where the petals represent or symbolize the days of creation or the "kingdoms" of earth or enlightenment. We don't know, and as far as we can tell, no one else knows either.

For your labyrinth walk, you can step into each petal one at a time. They become a container within a container. Perhaps a guardian will come to you or a mythic figure with a message just for you in each petal. Who knows? Kim has six iconic figures who visit her when she walks the labyrinth, one for each petal.

Step into each petal if you like. Try to be aware and grounded. See what happens.

Next Step in Your Journey

When you are ready, you might say a thank you to the labyrinth or to yourself or the land—or everything. Then walk out how you came in: You are following the same path out.

Once you get to the end of the path again and you are about to step out to continue your day, you might turn around to observe the labyrinth one more time and express your gratitude. Kim always gives a little bow.

There you are! See how simple that is?

Go forth and walk. We hope you enjoy.

Kim & Mario Walk Labyrinths

In the rest of the book, you will find some labyrinths we've walked. We write about these not because they are particularly special: all labyrinths are special, and we enjoyed walking these. ☺ But we wanted to show you the variety of labyrinths in communities these days.

Labyrinths have been built and continue to be built in parks, on school grounds, outside of churches and synagogues, and on private land. You can find out where labyrinths are by looking them up on the World-Wide Labyrinth Locator. Not all labyrinths are on the locator (ours aren't), so ask around if you can't find any in your area. There might be a private one in or near your neighborhood. Always ask before going to a private labyrinth, of course.

Although we love exploring labyrinths that are new to us, we enjoy going back to favorites again and again at different times of the day and year and seeing what is the same and what is different about each experience.

Grace Cathedral, San Francisco, California

The first labyrinths we walked were ones we made in the sand on the beach in Oregon. The first labyrinths we walked that were made by someone else were the ones inside and outside the Grace Cathedral in 1997. The installation of the labyrinth in the Grace Cathedral was in many ways the beginning of the modern labyrinth movement in the United States.

We write about our experience here more extensively earlier in the book. Both the inside and outside one are Medieval Chartres replicas.

The Grotto Labyrinth, Portland, Oregon

The Grotto is a Catholic sanctuary on 62 bucolic acres in Portland's Madison South neighborhood that opened in May of 1924. It's now over a hundred years old!

It began when Ambrose Mayer, a young boy in Canada, prayed for his sick pregnant mother. He promised to do something for the church if his mother was saved. His mother and his baby sister survived. He later became Friar Ambrose Mayer and was sent to Portland to serve. That's when he began to fulfill his promise to the church by creating the Grotto, which is formally called the National Sanctuary of Our Sorrowful Mother.

In the upper level of the gardens (accessed via an elevator), an 11-circuit labyrinth modeled after the Chartres labyrinth was built in 2010.

Kim first went to the Grotto before the turn of the century with her folks who were visiting from Michigan. The labyrinth wasn't there then, but we enjoyed the gardens on the upper level with the towering fir trees all around them. Kim loved it because she couldn't tell they were in the city.

Years later, once the labyrinth was installed, Kim and Mario started visiting regularly. We got an annual pass so we could come as often as we wanted. The labyrinth is in a quiet part of the gardens, far from the chapel and elevator, and it's often empty and quiet.

Sometimes Kim would drive to Portland just to visit the Grotto. She started writing her novel *Queendom* there while sitting in the church on the lower level, gazing up at the arch above the altar where the words BEHOLD THY MOTHER were written. The Grotto and its labyrinth is one of Kim's favorite places in the world. The chapel on the upper level affords a spectacular view of Mount St. Helens.

Labyrinth at the Menucha Retreat and Conference Center, Corbett, Oregon

Volunteers created this labyrinth out of stone and brick over a two year period (2007/2008) on Menucha's lovely acreage that is accessed down a long windy dirt road. The Center sits above the Columbia River, and the labyrinth is surrounded by grass, trees, and flower gardens. Permission to walk the labyrinth is freely given at the retreat office.

We can't remember exactly when we started visiting it, but Kim brought friends to this labyrinth frequently. During one of her first visits there, a huge gorgeous stag stepped out of the woods and watched her and her friends for a moment, and then it was gone. Kim often visited this labyrinth on her way home from the Grotto in Portland.

The Center says that their labyrinth is Medieval. They write the labyrinth takes the seven circuits "from the Classical and sets them in a more Medieval framework of a circle quartered by a cross."

Cretan Labyrinth at Trout Lake Abbey/White Mountain Druid Sanctuary, Trout Lake, Washington

Kim made the trip to the Abbey/Sanctuary many times before the labyrinth was built, to attend workshops and pick up fresh organic eggs. The Abbey is situated at the base of Mount Adams and is an organic farm as well as an abbey and retreat space.

They write, "Our mission is to support the well-being of all living things and provide a space for people to explore whatever spiritual path to which they are drawn."

One day we came for a visit and we discovered their new labyrinth made from large stones. When walking it, one has an amazing view of Mount Adams. We've been there when Mount Adams was on fire, and the view from the labyrinth was quite spectacular. This large labyrinth feels as solid as the hills surrounding it.

It is Cretan design and has seven circuits.

Mabel Dodge Luhan House Labyrinth, Taos, New Mexico

The Mabel Dodge Luhan House in Taos is one of Kim's favorite places on the planet. We stumbled upon it in the nineties when we were desperately looking for a place to stay in Taos that didn't use pesticides.

We drove from Kingman, Arizona, to Taos, arriving near midnight. We went slowly down a long dirt road and wondered if we had taken a wrong turn. Then our headlights spotlit a mermaid swimming across a cream-colored wall. We knew we were headed to the right place. In the morning, we awakened to a New Mexican blue sky day, and Kim felt like she had come home.

We visited and stayed in the house many times. It is always a sweet and profound experience to be in this space.

The rock labyrinth was created in 2009 and is not far from the house. It is Classical 7-circuit concentric.

Labyrinth at Ghost Ranch Conference Center, Abiquiu, New Mexico

This is another favorite place of ours in New Mexico. Georgia O'Keeffe visited and then lived here (on a few acres on Ghost Ranch) for some years. One can see Pedernal from Ghost Ranch and imagine all the hours O'Keeffe spent looking at it and painting it.

The 11-circuit Chartres-like labyrinth was built in 1998, years after O'Keeffe was gone. It is a bit away from the buildings with glorious views of red rock, near to the banks of the often dry river. Rocks are at the center instead of petals. It always feels very peaceful. The walk to it can be quite hot when the sun is up and out.

According to the Labyrinth Resource Group, this labyrinth was built by Lauren Artress, mother of the modern labyrinth movement, and Jean Richardson.

Sacred Heart Parish Labyrinth, Anderson, California

For a decade or more, we drove to a place in the Sonoran Desert just outside Tucson called Endicott West. (Fifteen years later, we bought the place, and it became the Old Mermaids Sanctuary.) Anderson, California, was a third of the way from our home in Washington state to Endicott West. We stayed at an environmentally friendly lodge there.

As usual, the first time we visited, we looked for a labyrinth. We found one close by, drove to it, and walked it. It always looked worse for wear, but walking it helped ground us and find a temporary home in Anderson along the banks of the Sacramento River. We haven't been for a few years, and we've heard it has deteriorated some. But we remember it fondly.

Beth Shalom Temple Center, Green Valley, Arizona

We love visiting this sweet town not far from the border and about an hour from where we live now. They have beautiful gardens and more labyrinths than we expected. This labyrinth situated next to the synagogue was built in September of 2018 by the Beth Shalom Temple Men's Group. It's described on their website as "a 6-circuit Jericho design with seven walls of river rock." Lots of birds seemed to be gathered around as we walked.

    Just as there is no standard way of walking a

labyrinth, there is no standard way of building one. This example, like so many others, shows the creativity and think-outside-the-box spirit that so many labyrinth builders bring to their projects.

Boyce Thompson Arboretum, Superior, Arizona

We usually leave the house long before dawn when it is still dark to get to this arboretum which is not far from Phoenix. The arboretum actually has two labyrinths. One is tiny and a bit difficult to find. The one pictured here is at the end of the forest, before the desert begins. It's Classical/Cretan 7-circuit. It's made from large stones, and it doesn't take long to walk it. Often it sounds as though we are surrounded by birds. Usually no human bothers us while we are walking it.

Corpus Christi Catholic Church, Tucson, Arizona

This Medieval 11-circuit labyrinth isn't far from our house, and it's probably the first one we walked in Tucson. It's in a nice spot with good views of the blue sky and the mountains. It is built on red gravel which means it is quite vocal when walking it. Mario sometimes imagines it is talking to him with impressive insistence, like it has something important to say. It was built in March 2009 by Ron and Helen Russell and parishioners. The bench in the center is a nice touch, inviting walkers to sit and contemplate their surroundings.

Episcopal Church of St. Matthew, Tucson, Arizona

This Medieval 8-circuit labyrinth was built in 2015. Just off Old Spanish Trail, it sits almost right up against the church and off the parking lot. When we visited, it seemed that a dog either lived on the residence or was frequently using the gravel as a kind of dog kitty litter, unfortunately. That did spoil the walk a bit. Nevertheless a beautifully designed and executed labyrinth.

Franciscan Renewal Center, Scottsdale, Arizona

For many years, Kim's parents lived part-time in Scottsdale. We tried to visit them every winter. Being in the Phoenix area often exhausted Kim and trying to navigate family relationships always exhausted her, so she looked for places she could go—close by—to catch her breath and get her ground again. The Franciscan Renewal Center was just the place. Walking their Classical 7-circuit labyrinth was always the crowning touch for the visit.

Grace St. Paul's Episcopal Church, Tucson, Arizona

Walking this Chartres-like 11-circuit labyrinth outside this busy community church can sometimes make one feel a bit exposed and vulnerable. The church is on one side, the road on another, and a portico on another. The portico provides shelter from the sun, so the unhoused (and probably others) hang out there. One time we visited and didn't quite finish the walk because a couple of the people were screaming and yelling. It is one of the very few times we've left without finishing the walk. It's a fabulous place, though, with everyone welcome.

Kim Antieau and Mario Milosevic

Prestige Assisted Living at Green Valley, Arizona

This Classical 7-circuit labyrinth is right next to the Desert Meadows Park with its exquisite desert gardens managed by the Green Valley Gardeners. It's fun to walk the labyrinth and then walk the gardens. There's no shade on the labyrinth, so we try to go early in the morning. Plenty of shade in the park. This was built in May 2017.

St. Francis in the Valley Episcopal Church, Green Valley, Arizona

This small sheltered labyrinth in Green Valley was dedicated in May 2007. It is close to the road and parking lot, but this didn't ruin the experience. It was a nice walk. And we always enjoy being in Green Valley. They call it a Medieval Petite Chartres.

Highland Vista Neighborhood Association Labyrinth, Tucson, Arizona

This is one of our favorite labyrinths. When we first drove up to it, we almost didn't get out of the car. It is in a kind of nondescript park, and this Classical labyrinth looked quite small. But we had come all this way across town, so we got out and walked over to it. As we looked around, we realized that nearly every stone had artwork on it. There was a plaque explaining that anyone was free to add a rock.

It was designed and built by Eduardo Atjian II in August 3, 2020. According to news articles, Atjian got the idea during the isolation of the pandemic as a way to help the neighborhood come together to create something beautiful and be safe at the same time.

As we very slowly walked the labyrinth, we felt that sense of community. Every stone had something beautiful and uplifting to convey. From this experience we learned not to judge a labyrinth by our first impressions.

Immanuel Presbyterian Church, Tucson, Arizona

This labyrinth was installed in September 2007. When we visited the property we couldn't find the labyrinth on our own. We walked all over the property. Mario finally went inside and asked about it. A kind woman took us on a bit of a trek to a path that eventually led to the labyrinth. It is big and well-done. It was apparently an Eagle Scout project. Unfortunately, a tiny dog in a nearby house barked constantly and loudly the entire time we walked the labyrinth. We felt sorry for anyone who lived nearby; the barking was something we were unable to ignore. The design is Roman 7-circuit.

Episcopal Church of the Apostles, Oro Valley, Arizona

This is a large Man in the Maze labyrinth just outside the church. It was established around 2000. A woman who had helped build it came out while we were walking and talked to us for a while. She said that the Man in the Maze is the emblem of the Tohono O'odham Nation of Arizona and that the labyrinth symbolizes the Journey of Life. She seemed very proud of her contribution to the building of it and glad we were walking it. It is built on gravel so it was noisy, but it was a lovely walk, nevertheless.

Rio Vista Natural Resource Park, Tucson, Arizona

It took us a bit to find this labyrinth in the park. When we did, we were surprised at how big it was. Such a roomy labyrinth. It seemed like it was made for giants.

A woman was there with a small boy who ran around the labyrinth with the woman chasing him. We always like seeing children at our walks. This place was eerie and peaceful.

The design is Contemporary 7-circuit.

Sanctuary Cove Labyrinth, Base of Tucson Mountains, Arizona

We had to drive a while to find this Classical labyrinth, created in 2009. The address says Tucson, but it is far out of town at the base of the Tucson Mountains. This one seemed tailor-made for little people. It was a good example of making do with the space that was available. The views and setting are spectacular.

St John on the Desert Presbyterian Church, Tucson, Arizona

This Classical 7-circuit labyrinth was put into operation in 2015. It feels quite isolated, and the gravel makes it a noisy walk. However, it was a pleasant and peaceful walk with a long path to get to the labyrinth that felt almost like an extension of the main design.

Saint Philip's in the Hills, Tucson, Arizona

We're guessing that when this church was built it was way out in the desert. Now it is squarely in the city with noisy busy streets on two sides. The labyrinth was apparently built in 2012. A wall on two sides protects it from the road, but it doesn't alleviate the traffic noise.

It's a Medieval 9-circuit octagonal labyrinth, based on the Amiens design. The Amiens design replicates the labyrinth in the French Cathedral Notre Dame d'Amiens. The path goes around a large octagon fountain structure.

It's the only labyrinth Kim has actually lost her way on—twice. The bricks that make up the path are very similar in color to the background bricks. Mario also lost his way a couple of times. No matter, we both got to the center eventually, and found our way out!

Sunrise Chapel Labyrinth, Tucson, Arizona

This adorable Classical 5-circuit labyrinth is a bit off the beaten path but easily found near the parking lot. It was established October 2016.

The trees offer good shade, which means we can walk it fairly comfortably even in hot weather. It seems to fit into the landscape so well that it almost doesn't even seem built. It's as though it grew there all on its own. A unique experience, unlike any other labyrinth we've ever walked.

Rincon Congregational United Church of Christ, Tucson, Arizona

This sweet labyrinth was created by the Rincon Congregational UCC in 2016. We love visiting this one because the church has so many beautiful signs of acceptance for everyone, especially those often shunned by society. It just feels good to be in a place where no one is shouting; everyone is loving.

They call it a Classical 7-circuit design. However it seems the builders went their own way, not particularly loyal to any traditional design. Walking it brought an appreciation of their creativity and independence.

Unity of Tucson, Tucson, Arizona

This Classical labyrinth was created in 2001. The day we came to walk it, other people were just leaving. This was unusual. Mostly we never run into anyone else when we are walking. While we were there, a coyote ran around in a gully below and then up on the road. We thought this was a very Sonoran desert labyrinth experience.

It features glazed ceramic bricks to define the path, a material we don't often see in labyrinths, once again showing there is no right way to design and build a labyrinth.

The Old Mermaids Sanctuary Labyrinth, Tanque Verde, Arizona

This is our Chartres-like 11-circuit labyrinth, created in 2019, the year we moved to Arizona. We wrote about how to do it in *Kim and Mario Build a Labyrinth and So Can You.*

The following year, we created a Cretan type labyrinth next to it. It has been a profound experience to watch them change over the years and to walk them again and again.

Vegetation grows between the rocks. Ants make colonies, dislodging the rocks. Birds knock the stones aside to get at bugs and seeds underneath. We've seen coyotes out there along with rabbits and roadrunners. Our labyrinths are living, breathing things, always changing, always different. We wouldn't have it any other way.

About the Authors

Kim Antieau is a writer and photographer who lives in the desert Southwest of the United States with her husband, writer Mario Milosevic. Her books include *Ruby's Imagine, Church of the Old Mermaids,* and *Jigsaw Woman.* She is a trained Veriditas labyrinth walk facilitator.

Mario Milosevic's books include the novels *Labor Days, Splitting, The Last Giant,* and *Terrastina and Mazolli,* the poetry collection *Animal Life,* and the story collection *Mostly Invisible.* mariowrites.com.

Together they have written *Kim and Mario Build a Labyrinth and So Can You.*